NASTY

BUGS

Poems Selected by
Lee Bennett Hopkins

Illustrated by
Will Terry

 DIAL BOOKS FOR YOUNG READERS
An imprint of Penguin Group (USA) Inc.

*To future entomologists
who love learning more
about nasty bugs*

—L.B.H.

For Magdalena Ingersol

—W.T.

Thanks are due to the following for use of works especially commissioned for this collection: Curtis Brown, Ltd. for *Boll Weevil* by Rebecca Kai Dotlich, copyright © 2012 by Rebecca Kai Dotlich; *Ode to a Dead Mosquito* by Lee Bennett Hopkins, copyright © 2012 by Lee Bennett Hopkins; *Lice* by Amy Ludwig VanDerwater, copyright © 2012 by Amy Ludwig VanDerwater. All reprinted by permission of Curtis Brown, Ltd.

All other commissioned works are used by permission of respective poets, who control all rights: Cynthia S. Cotten for *Stink Bug*; Douglas Florian for *The Giant Water Bug*; Kristine O'Connell George for *Bedbug Has a Bite to Eat*; Fran Haraway for *Cockroach*; X. J. Kennedy for *Colorado Potato Beetle*; Kami Kinard for *Tick-Tock Tick*; Michele Krueger for *Barbed and Dangerous*; J. Patrick Lewis for *Spoiled Rotten*; Rebecca Andrew Loescher for *Ode to Chigger*; Ann Whitford Paul for *Fly's Poem*; Alice Schertle for *Termite Tune*; Marilyn Singer for *Disagreeable Fleas*; April Halprin Wayland for *Fire Ants*.

DIAL BOOKS FOR YOUNG READERS
A division of Penguin Young Readers Group

Published by the Penguin Group

Penguin Group (USA) Inc., 375 Hudson Street, New York, New York 10014, U.S.A. * Penguin Group (Canada), 90 Eglinton Avenue East, Suite 700, Toronto, Ontario M4P 2Y3, Canada (a division of Pearson Penguin Canada Inc.) * Penguin Books Ltd, 80 Strand, London WC2R 0RL, England * Penguin Ireland, 25 St Stephen's Green, Dublin 2, Ireland (a division of Penguin Books Ltd) * Penguin Group (Australia), 250 Camberwell Road, Camberwell, Victoria 3124, Australia (a division of Pearson Australia Group Pty Ltd) * Penguin Books India Pvt Ltd, 11 Community Centre, Panchsheel Park, New Delhi—110 017, India * Penguin Group (NZ), 67 Apollo Drive, Rosedale, Auckland 0632, New Zealand (a division of Pearson New Zealand Ltd) * Penguin Books (South Africa) (Pty) Ltd, 24 Sturdee Avenue, Rosebank, Johannesburg 2196, South Africa * Penguin Books Ltd, Registered Offices: 80 Strand, London WC2R 0RL, England

CIP Data is available.

Published in the United States by Dial Books for Young Readers, a division of Penguin Young Readers Group, 345 Hudson Street, New York, New York 10014 * www.penguin.com/youngreaders

Designed by Jason Henry

Manufactured in China * First Edition
ISBN: 978-0-8037-3716-7
1 3 5 7 9 10 8 6 4 2

Contents

Stink Bug by Cynthia S. Cotten   5

Fly's Poem by Ann Whitford Paul   6

Boll Weevil by Rebecca Kai Dotlich   9

Colorado Potato Beetle by X. J. Kennedy   10

Ode to a Dead Mosquito by Lee Bennett Hopkins   11

Fire Ants by April Halprin Wayland   12

Barbed and Dangerous by Michele Krueger   14

Disagreeable Fleas by Marilyn Singer   16

Spoiled Rotten by J. Patrick Lewis   18

Ode to Chigger by Rebecca Andrew Loescher   19

Lice by Amy Ludwig VanDerwater   20

Tick-Tock Tick by Kami Kinard   22

Termite Tune by Alice Schertle   25

Cockroach by Fran Haraway   26

Bedbug Has a Bite to Eat by Kristine O'Connell George   27

The Giant Water Bug by Douglas Florian   28

ABOUT THE Nasty Bugs   30

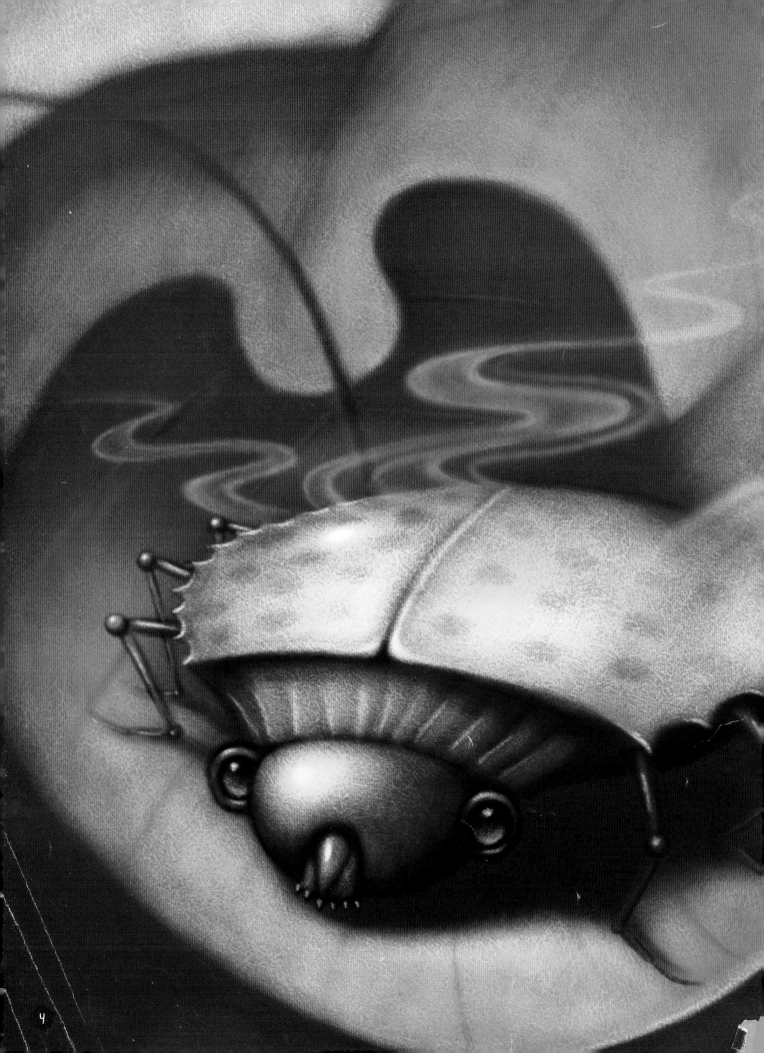

Stink Bug

When feeling threatened
or full of fear
some bugs
hiss
or sting
or bite.
Some skitter and scurry.
Some spread their wings in flight,
or curl up tight.
Some look scary,
some taste bad,
some use camouflage
to blend in just right.

Not me.

Small, slow,
shield-shaped,
grayish-brown
or green—
I have a secret weapon:
a tiny gland on either side
of my underside
and a liquid,
pungent and powerful enough
to empty an entire room.

You think I'm joking?
Go ahead, then—
touch me.

Just be prepared
to hold
your nose.

by CYNTHIA S. COTTEN

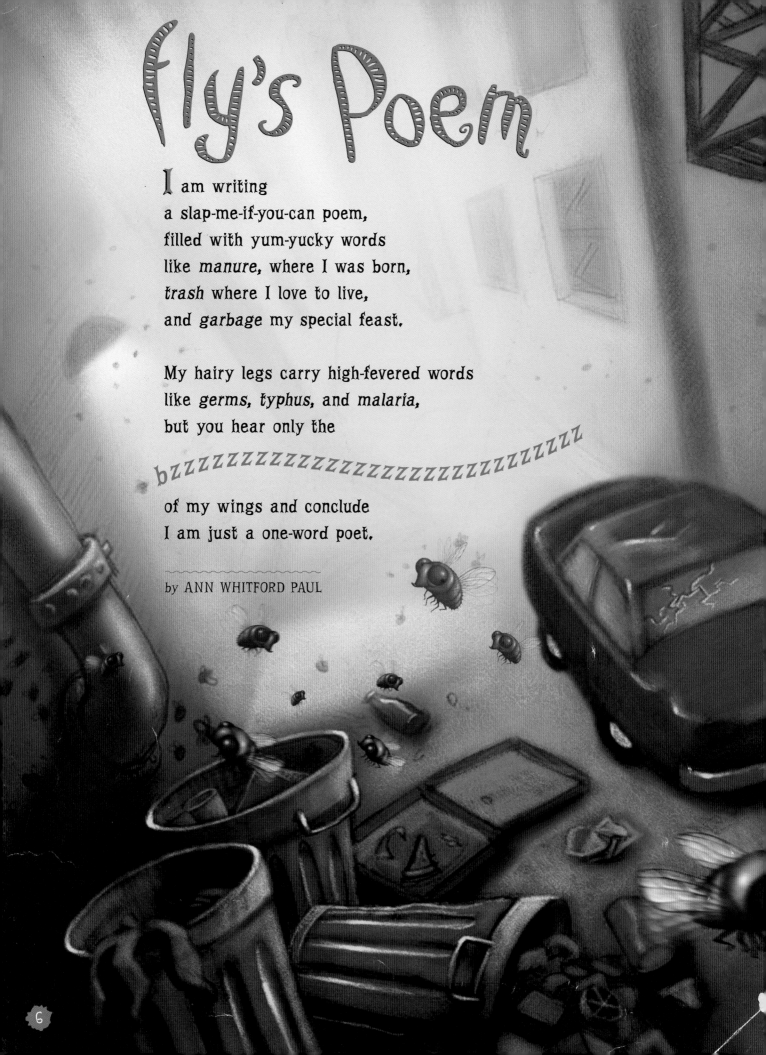

Fly's Poem

I am writing
a slap-me-if-you-can poem,
filled with yum-yucky words
like *manure*, where I was born,
trash where I love to live,
and *garbage* my special feast.

My hairy legs carry high-fevered words
like *germs*, *typhus*, and *malaria*,
but you hear only the

bzzzzzzzzzzzzzzzzzzzzzzzzzzzzzzzz

of my wings and conclude
I am just a one-word poet.

by ANN WHITFORD PAUL

Boll Weevil

I am an evil weevil,
a cotton-craving beetle
whose reputation's rotten
'cause I gobble crops of cotton,
       yes I do.

O, my crooked little legs
take my ugly little mouth
to the cotton way out West,
to the cotton of the South,
       it is true.

I am a creepy cotton thief,
born a Boll with one belief;
chew that cotton, chew a LOT,
(that's what baby Bolls
       are taught.)

O, I am an evil weevil,
a nibble-gnawing beetle,
but do not call me rotten,
it's my job to chomp on cotton,
       it is true.

by REBECCA KAI DOTLICH

Colorado Potato Beetle

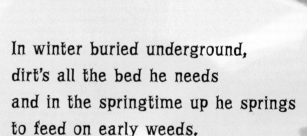

His other name's Potato Bug.
This munching desperado
infests our gardens coast to coast.
Not just in Colorado.

Ten stripes of black run down his back.
He wiggles orange legs,
and what is wonderful, his wife
can lay six hundred eggs.

In winter buried underground,
dirt's all the bed he needs
and in the springtime up he springs
to feed on early weeds.

Until a young potato plant
turns over a new leaf
and then he eats and eats and eats,
the nasty little thief.

He has a hard and slippery shell,
and sometimes this tough bug
when sprayed with an insecticide
will just shrug (if bugs shrug).

by X. J. KENNEDY

Ode to a Dead Mosquito

So—

You felt the need
to feed
a feast of blood
from me?

So—

You of little brain
didn't you know
I felt your sting
the instant you
began to drain?

So—

I whacked you.

SMACK!

You dropped.

So—

You did not have
an ounce to gain
you tried—
but did it all

in vain.

by LEE BENNETT HOPKINS

Fire Ants

*A*ll for one and one for all!—our tribal cry

Flood waters rise!
Quick, form a ball—
our larvae, pupae, eggs, and Mother Queen inside!

We roll this writhing globe,
take turns on top
so all breathe air, so all survive.

Trapping air in body hair,
even underwater,
we're alive.

We float this boat of bodies bobbing...BAM!
We've hit a tree! We swarm the trunk
and wait for rising rivers to recede.

All for one and one for all!—our tribal cry

At last—the end of rain!
We build a mound—
it rises two feet high on a soggy field of grain.

And if a passerby
comes near our new terrain?
It *will* feel pain.

Grasshopper, rat,
songbird, or cat—

All for one and one for all!
  —our tribal cry
this trespasser will **fry.**

by APRIL HALPRIN WAYLAND

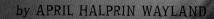

Barbed and Dangerous

An empty swarm
can do great harm
if happened on,
by chance.

They'll soon dispense
an armament to perform
a great war dance.

To protect their nest
to defend their young,
to save their queen
you will be stung;

becoming
victims
in the path
of wasp's aggressive,
vengeful wrath.

On marbled wings,
this vicious mob
delivers stings
that sorely throb.

It's best
to avoid
their nest.

by MICHELLE KRUEGER

Disagreeable fleas

These eager bugs hop,
      set up shop
in houses, yards,
      on St. Bernards.

They are fond of heat
They like backs, legs, and feet—
      places easy to bite.
They are never polite.

They find rats great to hitch,
      make all victims itch.
They drink blood, spread disease.

Can't we please get rid of fleas?

by MARILYN SINGER

Spoiled Rotten

I'm a maggot.
I'm a marvel
Of the larval generation.
I'm a comma
In a drama
Of disgusting devastation.

Multiply me!—
I'm a slimy
Bug, who's earned his reputation
As I've gotten
Spoiled rotten.

Want to see a demonstration?

by J. PATRICK LEWIS

Ode to Chigger

Oh, tiny, lumpy, ugly chigger,
it would be dreadful, were you bigger,
all hairy-red, with mouth that pinches—
how scary if you measured inches.
You hatch with six small legs for running,
then grow two more—for leaps most stunning,
grab onto something sweaty, smelly,
with thoughts of filling up your belly;
leave itchy spit—your thank-you present.
Oh, chigger, you are most unpleasant!

by REBECCA ANDREW LOESCHER

Lice

Ridiculous *Pediculus*
O tiny vampire louse
You crawl from head
          to head
              to head
from house
          to house
              to house.

Older than Columbus,
you reached the New World first.
Proof lies in two mummies' locks
whose life-blood quenched your thirst.
Now as we head off to school,
your nits stick in our hair.
Sesame seeds born crystal clear,
no one knows they're there.

Deep between our once clean sheets
you roam like mini mice.
When we share hats we're sharing you
like eggy leggy rice.

In seven days a batch will hatch,
drink human blood, turn brown.
In one more week they'll lay
   more eggs,
infesting one more town.

Stronger than insecticides,
the scourge of every head,
you're hard to ditch
you make us itch
but comb-by-comb
you're dead.

by AMY LUDWIG VANDERWATER

Tick-Tock Tick

The tick
tick-tock
ignoring the clock,
waits upon
a blade of grass.

It senses
heat
with questing feet
and hitchhikes on
the next to pass.

It does
not race.
With stealthy pace
it creeps through hair
and over skin.

It finds
a site
just right to bite.
With tiny teeth
it punctures in.

It then
imbeds
a needle-head.
Anesthetic
is injected.

Its host
won't feel
it steal-a-meal.
Thus it gorges
undetected.

The tick
tick-tock
ignoring the clock
sips for hours—
for days—nonstop.

It grows
from flat
to blood-filled fat.
When it's about
to pop—

it drops.

by KAMI KINARD

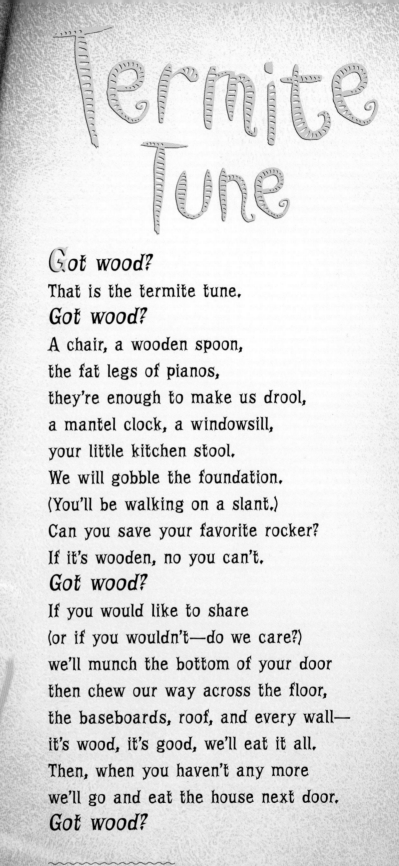

Termite Tune

Got wood?
That is the termite tune.
Got wood?
A chair, a wooden spoon,
the fat legs of pianos,
they're enough to make us drool,
a mantel clock, a windowsill,
your little kitchen stool.
We will gobble the foundation.
(You'll be walking on a slant.)
Can you save your favorite rocker?
If it's wooden, no you can't.
Got wood?
If you would like to share
(or if you wouldn't—do we care?)
we'll munch the bottom of your door
then chew our way across the floor,
the baseboards, roof, and every wall—
it's wood, it's good, we'll eat it all.
Then, when you haven't any more
we'll go and eat the house next door.
Got wood?

by ALICE SCHERTLE

Cockroach

The common cockroach family
Has quite a genealogy.
This tribe is tough; it perseveres.
It's lived three hundred million years.
So entomologists confess—
The cockroach is a great success!

Modern cockroaches are dwellers
Inside city wall and cellars,
Or they sleep beneath a sink.
Folks who won't approach them think
Cavemen should have sprayed the whole
Family tree for pest control!

by FRAN HARAWAY

Bedbug Has a Bite to Eat

I am nocturnal—your day is my night.
thus, I wait until you are tucked in tight
before I indulge in a morning snack.
Yet you call my simple meal an *attack!*
Such a nasty fuss! So much gripe and whine.
Exterminator?!? All I do is dine.

I'm not ruthless, vicious, nor malicious—
It's just that I find you
absolutely
　　　deeee licious.

by KRISTINE O'CONNELL GEORGE

The Giant Water Bug

The Giant Water Bug is big.
Up to four inches long.
Its pointed beak is very sharp.
Its legs are very strong.
Beneath the water motionless
This hunter likes to hide.
Onto its prey it loves to leap
Then holds on for the ride.
Its beak then pierces through its prey,
Injecting nasty stuff.
Enzymes melt the prey's insides
Until it's had enough.
The liquid that remains inside
The Water Bug will suck.
Ugh! Ugh! Ugh! Ugh!
Uck! Uck! Uck!

by DOUGLAS FLORIAN

About The
Nasty Bugs

....

Bedbugs

". . . your day is my night."

SCIENTIFIC NAME: *Cimex lectularius*

Bedbugs, small, nocturnal, wingless insects drain blood from humans and other warm-blooded hosts.

The bug pierces the skin with two hollow tubes. One tube injects saliva, the other withdraws blood. Bedbugs can drink three times their weight in one feed.

Bites usually cannot be felt until minutes or hours after an attack. After biting they leave small itchy bumps on the surface of skin. Bedbug infestations occur throughout the world. These nasty bugs have existed since prehistoric times.

....

Boll Weevil

". . . I gobble crops of cotton . . ."

SCIENTIFIC NAME: *Anthonomus grandis*

The boll weevil, a beetle that feeds on cotton buds and flowers, migrated to the United States from Mexico in the late 19th century. The nasty bug infested all cotton growing areas in the country by the 1920s, causing devastation to the cotton industry.

The bug causes damages amounting to about 300 million dollars each year.

Chigger

". . . all hairy-red with mouth that pinches . . ."

SCIENTIFIC NAME: *Trombicula alfreddugesi*

Chiggers, tiny, six-legged mites, cause more torment for their size than any other creature on earth. They are only about 1/20 of an inch long and travel rapidly.

In addition to attacking humans, they feed on a variety of snakes, turtles, birds, and small animals.

Chiggers burrow into skin inserting their mouthparts in skin pores or hair follicles. Intense itching occurs which is quite nasty to deal with.

....

American Cockroach

"This tribe is tough . . ."

SCIENTIFIC NAME: *Periplaneta americana*

The American cockroach, the largest of house-infesting roaches, are not only a nuisance but they can cause asthma in children.

Cockroaches hide during day and forage for food at night. When disturbed they flee rapidly. Adult roaches can live at least two to three months without food, a month without water. These nasty scavengers will eat almost anything, including paper, hair, cloth, book bindings, and dead insects.

....

Colorado Potato Beetle

"This munching desperado . . ."

SCIENTIFIC NAME: *Leptinotarsa decemlineata*

Feared by farmers, the Colorado potato beetle is a serious pest that feeds on potato stems preventing the production of tubers.

The bug was discovered in the late 1800s when it began destroying potato crops in Nebraska. Potato farmers find the bug quite nasty.

fire Ants

"All for one and one for all!"

SCIENTIFIC NAME: *Solenopsis invicta*

Thriving in mounds, fire ants will attack aggressively to bite and sting any intruder—including humans. One mound can host up to 500,000 of these nasty insects. Stings can produce symptoms such as localized pain and swelling to shock.

Twenty million people are stung by fire ants each year. At least three million have allergic reactions.

....

fleas

"They are never polite."

SCIENTIFIC ORDER: Siphonaptera

More than 2,000 species of fleas survive worldwide. These nasty clinging bloodsuckers attack a wide variety of warm-blooded hosts, including dogs, cats, chickens, mice, rats, squirrels, and humans. For every flea found on an animal there are many more developing in the home. Since fleas feed on blood they can cause anemia and even death if not treated. It is estimated that pet owners alone spend over one billion dollars annually to control flea infestation.

....

Housefly

"...bzzzzzzzzzzzzzzzzzzzzzzzzz..."

SCIENTIFIC NAME: *Musca domestica*

Among the most common insects houseflies can be found wherever there are humans. Females can lay up to 1,000 eggs during their life cycle of about two-three weeks. They are capable of spreading bacterial diseases such as food poisoning, typhoid, cholera, malaria, and dysentery.

Their super vision makes them sensitive to movement, enabling them to fly quickly at the first sign of danger. This makes these nasty insects difficult to swat.

Lice

"...you make us itch..."

SCIENTIFIC NAME: *Pediculus humanus capitis*

Each year millions of children are affected by head lice. Constant scratching can lead to skin irritation and even infection. Although head lice are not dangerous and do not spread disease, they are extremely contagious.

Recent studies show lice have been around for thousands of years, even being found on Egyptian mummies. Itching can be nasty.

....

Maggots

"...I've gotten/Spoiled rotten."

SCIENTIFIC ORDER: Diptera

Maggot is the common name for fly larvae. When flies lay eggs in moist, rotting waste, they hatch into this stage. Maggots travel in masses and are found in all kinds of decaying matter.

Hatched larvae burrow into the skin of cattle, sheep, deer, and humans, causing nasty lesions that can damage vital organs.

Maggots are also used in the field of medicine to clean open wounds.

....

Mosquitoes

"...to feed/a feast of blood..."

SCIENTIFIC ORDER: Diptera

Mosquitoes have been around for about 30 million years. That's a lot of nasty stings! Females must feed on the blood of mammals before their eggs can properly develop. They can drink as much blood as one and one-quarter times their own weight at a time.

Various species of the mosquito family can cause malaria, a disease causing about four million deaths worldwide annually; yellow fever, usually found in certain parts of Africa and South America; and other deadly diseases.

Stink Bug

"...be prepared/to hold/your/nose."

SCIENTIFIC FAMILY: Pentaomidae

Stink bugs, named for their ability to exude a foul smelling substance from a pore on each side of their thorax, are mainly plant feeders. With needlelike mouthparts they suck sap from buds, blossoms, pods, seeds, and many hosts, including trees, shrubs, weeds, vines, and cultivated crops.

Originally found in East Asia, these nasty predators were first reported in the United States in the late 1990s. They do not harm humans but they are a pest when found in homes.

....

Termites

"Got wood?"

SCIENTIFIC NAME: *Cryptotermes cauifrons*

Termites have existed for about 50 million years. Over 3,000 species live in colonies ranging in size from a few hundred to several million. Truly social, they feed, groom, and protect one another. The offspring of one generation aids parents in raising the next. These nasty creatures are strong enough to eat an entire house!

....

Ticks

"With tiny teeth/It punctures in."

SCIENTIFIC NAME: *Rhipicephalus sanguineus*

Ticks are arachnids like scorpions, spiders, and mites. Many species of ticks found worldwide are capable of spreading serious diseases. They attach firmly to their hosts as they suck blood, feed slowly, and go unnoticed for long periods of time while feeding.

Common ticks are the American dog tick and the blacklegged tick, also known as the deer tick, which causes Lyme disease, a serious bacterial illness which became known in 1975 in Lyme, Connecticut.

Wasps

"...you will be stung."

SCIENTIFIC ORDER: Hymenoptoeran

There are about 75,000 known species of wasps. They will only attack humans in defense, so it is important to leave a wasp nest alone. If a nest is disturbed, over 100 creatures can be unleashed, each capable of delivering several nasty stings. It is the female that stings; males do not have stingers.

Although some of the species are nuisances, yellow jackets and paper wasps prey on larvae that destroy crops. They also play a role in the pollination of flowers.

....

Giant Water Bug

"...Uck! Uck! Uck!"

SCIENTIFIC NAME: *Lethocerus americanus*

These giants are among the largest insects found in the United States and Canada. Some species can grow as long as 4 inches. Adult water bugs attack small animals such as tadpoles, salamanders, and small fish. They grasp and hold their prey with powerful forelegs.

Although water bugs are not dangerous to humans, they can give a nasty, painful bite. In some Asian countries they are eaten as a source of protein.